THE LITTLE BOOK OF
SEX
FACTS

An Hachette UK Company
www.hachette.co.uk

Summersdale Publishers Ltd
Part of Octopus Publishing Group Limited
Carmelite House
50 Victoria Embankment
LONDON
EC4Y 0DZ
UK

www.summersdale.com

Printed and bound in China

ISBN: 978-1-80007-632-7

THE LITTLE BOOK OF
SEX

FACTS

SADIE CAYMAN

summersdale

Introduction

Have you ever wondered how many people around the world are having sex right now? Or who the largest penis on record belongs to? Perhaps you're more interested in what the world's first vibrator was originally used for? Whatever arouses your interest, this candid collection of titillating trivia is guaranteed to hit the spot. So prepare yourself for a wild ride as the following pages equip you with everything you need to become a certified sexpert. Just maybe don't read this while you're at work!

EVERY DAY, THERE ARE
APPROXIMATELY 100
MILLION ACTS OF SEXUAL
INTERCOURSE GLOBALLY.
IN OTHER WORDS, AROUND
65,000 COUPLES ARE
HAVING SEX AT THIS
MOMENT AROUND
THE WORLD.

The average time a person spends kissing in their lifetime is 20,160 minutes; that's two whole weeks.

Sex helps you sleep better. During orgasm, the body releases endorphins which often have a sedative effect. This can lead to a deeper, better-quality sleep.

The oldest known evidence of condom use is a cave painting in Grotte des Combarelles in France, estimated to be 12,000-15,000 years old.

A single sperm contains 37.5 MB of DNA information – this means that one ejaculation is equivalent in data capacity to 62 MacBook Pro laptops.

According to research, one in three Britons keep the lights off during sex. The most common reasons are self-consciousness, inability to relax, or wanting to save money on bills.

SEMEN IS PACKED FULL OF
MULTIVITAMINS, INCLUDING
VITAMIN C, CALCIUM,
MAGNESIUM, POTASSIUM,
ZINC AND MUCH MORE!
STUDIES HAVE ALSO SHOWN
THAT INGESTING SEMEN CAN
HELP YOU SLEEP BETTER AND
EVEN ACT AS A NATURAL
ANTIDEPRESSANT.

Half an hour of sex is said to burn between 85 and 200 calories (the equivalent to 15 minutes on a treadmill).

The word "masturbate" comes from the Latin *manus*, hand, and *stuprare*, to make dirty. Despite its bad name, we now know that masturbation is in fact good for you.

According to a study published by the *American Academy of Sleep Medicine*, nearly 10 per cent of all dreams involve sex.

Women get erections too. The clitoris is made up of the same spongy erectile tissue as the penis, which expands and engorges with blood when aroused.

Eating ginger stimulates the feelings of excitement associated with sex. It elevates your heart rate, gets your blood flowing and makes you excited for the night ahead.

A 2017 STUDY FOUND THAT
STRAIGHT WOMEN HAVE
THE FEWEST ORGASMS.
OF THE STRAIGHT WOMEN
SURVEYED, 65 PER CENT
REPORTED HAVING
ORGASMS EVERY TIME THEY
HAVE SEX, COMPARED TO
95 PER CENT OF STRAIGHT
MEN AND 86 PER CENT OF
LESBIAN WOMEN.

While orgasm and ejaculation generally appear to coincide for men, they actually occur in rapid succession with orgasm coming slightly before – and some men can orgasm without ejaculating at all.

Research has shown that wearing socks during sex makes a woman more likely to orgasm. This is because most women find it easier to climax when they feel comfortable and relaxed.

The world's largest recorded penis belongs to American actor and television presenter Jonah Falcon, whose appendage measures 9.5 inches (24 cm) flaccid and 13.5 inches (34 cm) erect.

The vibrator was first widely used in the Victorian era by doctors who used them on their female patients as a cure for "hysteria".

It is estimated that 37-39 per cent of men globally are circumcised. As well as being a religious and cultural practice, circumcision is also performed for medical and cosmetic reasons.

THE CLITORIS IS ACTUALLY
MUCH BIGGER THAN IT
SEEMS. THE PART WE SEE
IS JUST THE TIP OF THE
ICEBERG, WITH A MUCH
LARGER WISHBONE-SHAPED
STRUCTURE THAT EXTENDS
UP TO 13 CM UNDERNEATH
THE SKIN.

Reports claim that the highest number of orgasms experienced in 1 hour by a woman is 134. The record for a man is 16.

A single human male produces enough sperm in two weeks to impregnate every fertile woman on the planet.

Russian woman Tatyana Kozhevnikova is reported to be the world record holder for lifting the most weights - 14 kg - with her vaginal muscles.

Sex can help clear a blocked nose. During intercourse, in addition to the erectile and labial tissues, the inner nose also swells.

Aerobic exercise that increases blood flow to the genital region, such as jogging, cycling or vigorous walking, will increase your libido.

UPPER PALEOLITHIC ART
DATING BACK 30,000
YEARS DEPICTS PEOPLE
USING DILDOS TO PLEASURE
THEMSELVES AND EACH
OTHER. THIS MEANS THAT
THE HUMAN RACE INVENTED
SEX TOYS LONG BEFORE
THE WHEEL.

The average man has 11 erections per day, and three to five erections during a full night's sleep.

Of all nations, the Greeks claim to have the most sex (87 per cent say they have sex once a week).

Adult actress Lisa Sparxxx set a world record in 2004 when she had sex with 919 men in less than 24 hours.

When sperm are first ejaculated, they can reach speeds of up to 28 miles per hour. That's about as fast as Usain Bolt can run.

Sex is an effective form of pain relief. During arousal and orgasm, the hypothalamus in the brain releases the feel-good hormone oxytocin, which can significantly reduce pain perception.

ACCORDING TO ONE STUDY,
SPAIN, BRAZIL, AND ITALY
PRODUCE THE BEST LOVERS.
THE ENGLISH WERE SAID TO
BE "TOO LAZY", THE SWEDES
"FINISHED TOO QUICKLY",
AND AMERICANS RANKED
IN THE MIDDLE.

The female orgasm lasts three times longer than the male orgasm, with the average female orgasm lasting for around 20 seconds compared to just 6 seconds for the average male.

The amount of semen produced with each ejaculation is one to two teaspoons. The average man will produce about 14 gallons or 1 trillion sperm in his lifetime.

Formicophilia is a sexual pleasure derived from the feeling of small insects crawling over the skin and/or stinging/biting the private parts.

American writer Philip Roth caused controversy in 1969 when he published *Portnoy's Complaint*, about a sex-obsessed, sexually frustrated teenager who masturbates using various props, including a piece of liver.

According to a study, 36 per cent of people under the age of 35 ditch the post-sex cuddle for checking their Facebook and Twitter accounts instead.

MEN FAKE ORGASMS TOO. ACCORDING TO *TIME OUT NEW YORK*'S 2014 STUDY, MORE THAN 30 PER CENT OF MEN HAVE FAKED AN ORGASM. SO IT ISN'T JUST LADIES USING THEIR ACTING SKILLS IN THE BEDROOM.

Most women need direct clitoral stimulation in order to reach orgasm and cannot orgasm from vaginal penetration alone.

La petite mort, or "the little death", is a French term used to describe the moment of physical and spiritual release just after orgasm.

There are only two physiological responses in a human body that cannot voluntarily stop once they have started: sneezing and orgasm.

Researchers from the University of California found that men who helped with the housework got 50 per cent more sex than those who did none.

The fear of having, seeing or thinking about an erection is called ithyphallophobia.

SOME WOMEN CAN HAVE
NIPPLEGASMS, ALTHOUGH
THEY'RE PRETTY RARE.
NIPPLE STIMULATION
RELEASES OXYTOCIN,
WHICH CAN CAUSE THE
CONTRACTIONS ASSOCIATED
WITH ORGASM. THIS BRINGS
MORE BLOOD FLOW TO THE
GENITALS AND CAN RESULT
IN THE BIG O.

Some modern languages have beautifully descriptive words for dildo, such as *consolador* (Spanish for "consoler"), and *cala goeg* (Welsh for "fake penis").

An apple a day can lead to better sex. According to one study, women who ate the fruit once a day enjoyed a more regular and fulfilling sex life.

A 2014 study showed the average man thinks about sex 19 times a day, while women think about it ten times a day.

The clitoris has over 8,000 nerve endings - that's the greatest concentration in the entire body and double the number of nerve endings found in the penis.

The ancient Egyptians used dried crocodile dung as a contraceptive, as it contains spermicidal properties. They also used honey and condoms made of fabric.

SEX CAN LEAD TO A MORE
REGULAR MENSTRUAL CYCLE.
RESEARCH HAS FOUND
THAT WOMEN WHO HAD
SEX AT LEAST ONCE A WEEK
EXPERIENCED LESS PAINFUL,
MORE REGULAR PERIODS.

According to special research from the *British Medical Journal*, the more orgasms you have, the longer you're likely to live.

The reason semen sometimes has a bleach-like smell is due to the chemical spermine – a natural disinfectant that buffers the sperm from vaginal acids.

In Thailand, males are offered free vasectomies on the King's birthday. Often, over 1,000 are performed in his honour.

The G-spot, a highly sensitive area of the vagina, is named after Dr Ernst Gräfenberg. His research found that attention to this area could trigger powerful orgasms and female ejaculation.

Men have a G-spot too. The prostate has been dubbed the "male G-spot" due to its high concentration of nerve endings. And it seems the secret is out too, as sales of prostate massagers have been on the rise in recent years.

RESEARCH HAS SHOWN
THAT MORE PEOPLE PREFER
COFFEE TO SEX. A SURVEY
OF OVER 7,000 PEOPLE
SHOWED THAT 51 PER CENT
OF THEM SAID THEY COULD
GO LONGER WITHOUT SEX
THAN THEY COULD WITHOUT
A CUP OF COFFEE.

Sex is a great natural beauty treatment for women. It helps produce oestrogen, which makes women's hair shinier and gives their skin a natural glow.

According to a survey, the most popular sexual fantasy in the UK is threesomes, with 20 per cent of women and 30 per cent of men wanting to try it out.

According to the *Durex Global Sex Survey*, the average age for losing your virginity is 17 years old.

A man's testicles can increase by 50 per cent in size when he's aroused.

Kissing is good for your oral health as it increases salivary flow, which helps to clean your teeth and neutralize harmful acids that cause tooth decay.

WHEN IT COMES TO
NOTCHES ON THE BEDPOST,
THE CHINESE TOP THE POLLS
WITH AN AVERAGE OF 19
LOVERS PER LIFETIME. THE
VIETNAMESE HAVE THE
LEAST WITH AN AVERAGE OF
JUST TWO AND A HALF.

In 2013, a couple in Thailand broke the record for the world's longest kiss with a smooch that lasted 58 hours, 35 minutes and 58 seconds.

The most common out-of-the-bedroom spot for couples to have sex is in a car.

A university study has shown that straight females are just as aroused by watching erotica involving only women as they are by watching erotica involving both sexes.

Kellogg's Corn Flakes were actually invented as part of an anti-masturbation crusade. John Harvey Kellogg, one of the loudest anti-masturbation campaigners, believed that a healthy diet would curb sexual desire.

Scientists believe that the head of the human penis exists so it can "scoop" out any competing sperm that might be inside their partner's vagina, therefore increasing the man's chances of procuring offspring.

WHEN DR STUART MELOY
PUT AN ELECTRODE IN A
WOMAN'S SPINE TO CURE
HER BACK PAIN, SHE HAD
AN ORGASM. HE THEN
TRIED TO MARKET THE
"ORGASMATRON", A PUSH-
BUTTON DEVICE PROVIDING
REMOTE-CONTROLLED
INSTANT PLEASURE.

In humans, lips are more sensitive than genitals, and 100 times more sensitive than the tips of the fingers.

Of all the body parts – in both men and women – the clitoris is the only one that exists solely for pleasure.

Some people are allergic to semen – leading to itching and burning sensations. Even unluckier is to be one of those rare men who are allergic to their own semen.

Sex and chocolate have similar effects on the brain. Just like sexual arousal, the consumption of chocolate increases dopamine, triggering the brain's craving and reward centres.

Women generally make more noise than men during sex. Survey results reveal that reasons for making noise include expressing pleasure, boosting their partner's self-esteem and relieving boredom.

EUNUCHS IN IMPERIAL
CHINA OFTEN ROSE TO THE
TOP POSITIONS IN SOCIETY.
TRADITIONALLY A EUNUCH
WOULD KEEP HIS GENITALS
IN A JAR ON A HIGH SHELF,
AND AFTER DEATH, THE JAR
WOULD BE BURIED WITH
HIM, SO THAT HE COULD BE
REINCARNATED AS A NON-
CASTRATED MAN.

Sperm makes a great anti-wrinkle cream as it contains proteins that tighten the skin and give you an instant lift.

Breasts can swell up to 25 per cent bigger when aroused, making them super-sensitive.

The clitoris never stops growing. By the time a woman reaches her 30s, her clitoris is four times larger than it was at puberty.

The US state of Minnesota specifies that it is illegal for a man to have sex with a live fish; it says nothing about dead fish.

Despite many people using it as a common excuse to avoid sex, sex can actually relieve a headache as orgasm releases the tension, which restricts blood vessels in the brain.

ACCORDING TO A STUDY, PEOPLE TEND TO PREFER CHEESE TO ORAL SEX. EVERY YEAR COLUMBIA UNIVERSITY ASKS SOON-TO-BE GRADUATES IF THEY'D GIVE UP CHEESE IN FAVOUR OF ORAL SEX, AND EVERY YEAR THE SENIORS OVERWHELMINGLY CHOOSE CHEESE.

For both men and women, the heart rate averages 140 beats per minute at the moment of orgasm. That's considered a tachycardia (a rapid heartbeat).

A teaspoon of semen contains between five and 25 calories.

In the Aztec culture, avocados were considered so sexually powerful that virgins were restricted from contact with them.

Around 500–1,000 deaths occur per year as a result of auto-erotic asphyxiation, the intentional self-restriction of oxygen for the purposes of sexual arousal.

The Romans had three different words for types of kisses: *osculum* – a kiss on the cheek; *basium* – a kiss on the lips; *savolium* – a deep kiss.

RESEARCH HAS FOUND
THAT PEOPLE WHO SLEEP
ON THEIR STOMACHS HAVE
MORE SEX DREAMS. THIS IS
BECAUSE SLEEPING IN THIS
POSITION PUTS PHYSICAL
PRESSURE ON THE GENITALS
WHICH THEN TRANSFERS
INTO OUR DREAMS.

The average length of an erect penis is between 5 and 6 inches (12.5 cm to 15 cm). When flaccid, penis size averages around 3.5 inches (9 cm).

A study in the *Journal of Sexual Medicine* found that the average duration from the beginning of vaginal penetration until ejaculation was just over 5 minutes.

"Cat-heads" is a slang expression, described in Francis Grose's 1785 *Dictionary of the Vulgar Tongue* as a "sea phrase", for a woman's breasts.

Men who smoke have twice the risk of developing erectile dysfunction as non-smokers, with the link being strongest in younger men.

During the Victorian era, when public standards of morality were extremely strict, there were up to 80,000 prostitutes working in London.

FUNDAWEAR, FROM DUREX AUSTRALIA, ALLOWS LOVERS TO MOVE THEIR FINGERS ON AN APP TO TRANSMIT VIBRATIONS DIRECTLY ONTO THEIR PARTNERS' UNDERWEAR, IN AN INNOVATION THAT COULD BRING A LITTLE MORE PLEASURE INTO LONG-DISTANCE RELATIONSHIPS.

Non-lubricated condoms are distributed among the armed forces as emergency water holders which have the capacity to hold about a gallon of water.

In a global survey, more than a fifth of people would rather go out with their friends than have sex. Ten per cent would rather play sport or go shopping.

Taco Bell's "Chilito" changed its name to the "Chili Cheese Burrito" when it was discovered that *chilito* in Spanish means "small penis".

👄 In several countries, some new brides place tiny bags containing chicken's blood into the vagina prior to intercourse to prove the hymen was intact before marriage.

👄 The sex icon Marilyn Monroe had problems reaching orgasm – she told a friend that she had never had an orgasm with any of her three husbands or her many famous lovers.

DURING THE FIRST WORLD
WAR, MEMBERS OF THE
BRITISH SECRET INTELLIGENCE
SERVICE DISCOVERED YOU
COULD USE SEMEN AS
INVISIBLE INK. THEY STOPPED
USING IT AFTER THEY
REALIZED HOW BADLY IT
SMELLED WHEN IT GOT OLD.

Because there is an increase in blood circulation around the genitals during a woman's period, she may experience more powerful orgasms during this time.

Having at least four orgasms a week can apparently reduce a man's chances of getting prostate cancer.

Like the eye, the vagina is a self-cleaning organ, so you don't have to put anything up the passage to clean it.

Humans have pubic hair because it lessens friction during sex and prevents the transmission of bacteria. It is also theorized that the hair may also trap secretions that hold pheromones.

Having sex at least once a week can lower a man's risk of heart disease by 30 per cent, stroke by 50 per cent and diabetes by 40 per cent.

IN ONE STUDY, RESEARCHERS
FOUND WOMEN WHO HAD
A STRONGER SENSE OF
SMELL HAD MORE FREQUENT
ORGASMS. IN ANOTHER
STUDY, RESEARCHERS FOUND
THOSE WHO HAD LOST THEIR
SENSE OF SMELL REPORTED
LOWER SEX DRIVES.

Approximately 70 per cent of men refuse to have sex during their partner's period.

Although any body part or item of clothing may be an object of sexual fetishism, the shoe and the foot are the two most common fetishes in Western society.

According to research, the average sex session comprises 100 to 500 thrusts.

According to a survey conducted by sex toy company TENGA, Beyoncé and Brad Pitt are the two most-masturbated-to celebrities.

The *Kama Sutra* states that a ram's or goat's testicle boiled in sweetened milk can stimulate sexual desire.

THE FIRST PENIS PUMP WAS
INVENTED BY GEDDINGS
DAVID OSBON, AN
AUTOMOBILE AND TYRE
PROFESSIONAL. HE TOOK
WHAT HE KNEW ABOUT
MECHANICS AND APPLIED IT
TO THE ERECTION, CREATING
AN AID FOR ERECTILE
DYSFUNCTION WHICH HE
SOLD TO THE MASSES.

Women with a PhD are twice as likely to be interested in a one-night stand as those with a bachelor's degree.

In ancient China, drinking mercury or lead after sex was believed to prevent pregnancy; sadly, it often resulted in sterility or death.

A *Cosmopolitan* magazine survey found that foreplay between the average married couple tends to last between 14 and 17 minutes.

💋 After fingers and vibrators, candles are the phallic objects used most often by female masturbators. Unlit ones, hopefully.

💋 Overweight men have higher levels of the female estradiol hormone, which blocks male hormones and delays orgasm, meaning heavier men generally last longer in the bedroom.

ACCORDING TO A 2014
SURVEY, 76 PER CENT
OF MEN WATCH PORN,
COMPARED TO JUST 36 PER
CENT OF WOMEN. WOMEN
ALSO TEND TO TUNE IN WITH
THEIR PARTNER, WHILE MEN
ARE HAPPIER TO VIEW
PORN ALONE.

"Morning dew" is a slang term for vaginal lubrication, or sexual arousal, on waking up. "Morning wood" is the male equivalent.

Drinking too much coffee can deplete your sex drive. Too much caffeine overstimulates the adrenal glands, producing stress hormones that can have a negative impact on libido.

Masturbation and coitus interruptus, when the penis is withdrawn before ejaculation, are both sometimes referred to as "onanism", thanks to the biblical story of Onan, who "spilled his seed" deliberately on the ground.

Eating chilli, curry, or any other hot spice can act like an aphrodisiac by increasing heart rate and causing perspiration.

In a 1995 study in Switzerland, women were asked to sniff sweaty T-shirts. They consistently preferred the smell of men whose immune systems were different from their own.

AT LEAST HALF OF ALL
SEXUALLY ACTIVE PEOPLE
WILL HAVE A GENITAL HPV
(HUMAN PAPILLOMAVIRUS)
DURING THEIR LIVES; IN 90
PER CENT OF CASES, THE
IMMUNE SYSTEM WILL FIGHT
OFF THE DISEASE IN
TWO YEARS.

The eighteenth-century empress of Russia, Catherine the Great, was rumoured to employ professional "foot ticklers" to turn her on.

People who have just fallen in love have high levels of the neurotransmitter dopamine in their brains. This creates a pleasure rush similar to cocaine!

In Moroccan mythology, Qandisa is the goddess of lust who seduces men before driving them insane.

In thirteenth-century China, cock rings were commonly used and were made from the eyelids of goats. The goats' eyelashes were usually left on to add an extra bit of stimulation.

Wearing high heels may strengthen the pelvic muscles, which helps orgasm. In ancient Rome, only prostitutes were allowed to wear high heels.

FAR FROM A MODERN
INVENTION, THE DILDO
ACTUALLY DATES BACK
AROUND 30,000 YEARS,
AND THEY WERE ORIGINALLY
MADE FROM STONE. LATER
VERSIONS OF THE DILDO
WERE MADE FROM WOOD,
LEATHER AND EVEN DRIED
CAMEL DUNG.

Researchers at Rutgers University found that different regions of the brain become activated in response to stimulation of the vagina, cervix, clitoris and nipples.

Aristophanes, the fifth-century BCE Greek comedy playwright, devised 106 ways of describing the male genitals and 91 for those of the female.

On 16 February 1899, the President of France, Félix Faure, died in his office at the Élysée Palace while engaging in sexual activities.

👄 There are latex-free condoms made of polyurethane and polyisoprene for people with latex allergies.

👄 As protection against HIV, condoms make sex 10,000 times safer than unprotected sex.

IN ANCIENT GREECE,
THERE WAS AN ANNUAL
PROCESSION FOR THE GOD
DIONYSUS, WHEN THE MEN
CARRIED A LARGE PHALLUS.
THE CITY OF TYRNAVOS STILL
HOLDS AN ANNUAL PHALLUS
FESTIVAL DURING LENT.

Good listeners are often good in bed too. Someone who is engaged by your conversation and alert to conversational cues is more likely to be responsive to sexual needs.

In 401 CE, St Augustine wrote, "Nothing is so powerful in drawing the spirit of a man downwards as the caresses of a woman."

According to medical literature, there have been approximately 80 cases of a man being born with two penises.

According to ancient Jewish law, labourers should have intercourse with their wives twice a week; ass drivers only once a week.

Plant-based substances such as ginseng or vanilla, patchouli or musk scents are believed to stimulate sexual energy.

"PETTING PARTIES" WERE ALL THE RAGE IN THE 1920s. THESE WERE PLACES WHERE YOUNG MEN AND WOMEN COULD EXPLORE KISSING, TOUCHING, AND OTHER ASPECTS OF PHYSICAL CONTACT. BUT THERE WAS NO RISK OF GETTING CARRIED AWAY AS THE PARTIES INCLUDED EVERYTHING BUT SLEEPING TOGETHER.

Porn star Sonny Nash became record holder for the "Longest Time Spent Masturbating" after doing it for 10 hours and 10 minutes in May 2012.

In 953 CE, Princess Olga of Kiev introduced a law whereby men could return their wives if they found out they were not virgins, asking for monetary or material compensation.

Psychotria elata, a plant that grows in Central and South American tropical forests, has a flower that resembles two luscious, bright-red lipsticked lips - hence its nickname, Hooker's Lips.

💋 In Greek mythology, Aphrodite was born when the god Cronus cut off Uranus' genitals and threw them in the sea.

💋 The *Kama Sutra* contains 529 sex positions, including eight different types of oral sex.

RESEARCHERS AT THE
UNIVERSITY OF CALIFORNIA
FOUND THAT IT TAKES THE
MALE BRAIN ONLY A FIFTH
OF A SECOND TO DECIDE
IF SOMEONE IS SEXUALLY
ATTRACTIVE OR NOT –
CAUSING HIS PUPILS TO
DILATE AND HIS HEART RATE
TO ACCELERATE.

In 1837, there were over 50 pornographic shops on London's Holywell Street. This scurrilous address was lost when The Strand was widened in 1900.

Regular Pilates classes lead to better flexibility, more strength in the upper body and improved abdominal power - all good for trying different sex positions and making orgasms more intense.

A man's sweat glands release the hormone androstadiene, which can increase women's sexual arousal by up to 200 per cent.

The best-selling work of fiction of the fifteenth century was *The Tale of the Two Lovers*, an erotic novel by the man who later became Pope Pius II.

At the 2012 London Olympics, which lasted for 17 days, the athletes were provided with 150,000 free condoms – approximately 15 each.

IN 1919, BEFORE BEING
ELECTED PRESIDENT OF
AMERICA, FRANKLIN D.
ROOSEVELT IS BELIEVED TO
HAVE CREATED A SPECIAL
UNDERCOVER UNIT IN
THE NAVY. IT ATTEMPTED
TO ENTRAP GAY MEN BY
PERFORMING ORAL SEX ON
SUSPECTED HOMOSEXUALS.

Cervical caps made of gold or silver were once the most fashionable form of contraception - before science discovered Toxic Shock Syndrome.

The word aphrodisiac is named after Aphrodite, the Greek goddess of love, pleasure and procreation.

Kissing burns approximately two calories per minute.

The scent of vanilla - from a candle, cake or even ice cream - naturally boosts libido, creating feelings of calm and reducing inhibitions.

A poll found that 82 per cent of computer geeks claimed they put their partner's pleasure above their own (compared with only 41 per cent of fitness professionals).

KING EDWARD VII SPENT
SO MUCH TIME AT LE
CHABANAIS, A BROTHEL
IN PARIS, THAT A SPECIAL
LOVESEAT WAS MADE
FOR HIM; THIS WAS TO
SUPPORT HIS CONSIDERABLE
WEIGHT AS HE ENJOYED
THE SERVICES OF MANY
COURTESANS.

Thirty per cent of people aged 80 or over still have sexual intercourse.

Erectile dysfunction - or impotence - can be caused by stress, alcohol, smoking, diabetes or depression; it can be treated with therapy, medication or relaxing more.

Researchers found that 58 per cent of individuals who regularly watch porn felt more comfortable with their sexuality and with fulfilling their partner sexually.

Alcohol is not an aphrodisiac but it reduces inhibition, relaxing people and increasing their confidence; it also opens small blood vessels, making people feel flushed and warm.

Researchers from the Kinsey Institute found women today have less sex than their 1950s counterparts because we now "live in an age where there is little unfilled leisure time".

ONE OF THE FIRST
MAGAZINES TO DISPLAY
PHOTOGRAPHS OF FEMALE
NUDITY WAS THE FRENCH
MAGAZINE *LE FRISSON* AT
THE TURN OF THE TWENTIETH
CENTURY; FRENCH
MAGAZINES COMMONLY
PUBLISHED NUDES UNDER
THE GUISE OF NATURISM.

Syphilis was known as "the French Disease" in Italy and "the English Disease" in France.

In Losevo near St Petersburg, Russia, the Bubble Baba Challenge takes place every year. This is a race in which people raft blow-up sex dolls on the Vuoksa River.

"Shy nipples" are inverted – just like "innie" belly buttons. It's normal and doesn't affect stimulation.

👄 Women who masturbate regularly are more likely to experience an orgasm during sex with a partner.

👄 Massaging the heel just under the ankle bone can increase sensation in a man's penis.

IN ANCIENT ROME,
GLADIATORS' SWEAT WAS
USED AS AN APHRODISIAC.
THE SWEAT WAS SCRAPED
FROM THE GLADIATOR'S
SKIN AND MIXED WITH
DIRT AND OLIVE OIL
WHICH WAS THEN USED
AS A MOISTURIZER AND
LUBRICANT.

A 2012 study in Massachusetts established a link between high-fat diets and lower sperm counts.

Making a ring with your fingers and squeezing the base of the penis will prolong sex before orgasm.

People who develop a sexual attraction toward buildings and other inanimate objects call themselves "Objectum Sexuals". In 2007, one woman married the Eiffel Tower.

👄 When ovulating, women are more tolerant of chat-up lines and find high-testosterone men more attractive than at other stages of their cycle.

👄 The word "pornography" is derived from the Greek language, meaning "the writing of prostitutes".

AM ABEND, OR *IN THE EVENING*, IS ONE OF THE EARLIEST PORNOGRAPHIC FILMS, PRODUCED IN GERMANY IN 1910. IT STARTS WITH VOYEURISM, AS A MAN WATCHES A WOMAN MASTURBATING IN HER BEDROOM.

In 2012, the manager of the UK's Lake District's Damson Dene Hotel replaced the Bibles in guest rooms with copies of erotic bestseller *Fifty Shades of Grey*.

A researcher found, when interviewing hundreds of strippers, that "80 per cent of the job is talking".

In Victorian times, a prostitute was known as a "blowsy", and "blow" was slang for ejaculation. By the 1930s, the act of fellatio was known as a "blow job".

The juice of the silphium plant was a popular contraceptive in ancient Rome. It became extinct by the end of the first century CE.

Scientific studies have found that men with mild facial scars were more attractive to women than those without, but that the women didn't consider them suitable as marriage material.

IN 2008, ARCHAEOLOGISTS IN CYPRUS FOUND A SEVENTH-CENTURY CURSE INSCRIBED ON A LEAD TABLET THAT SAID, "MAY YOUR PENIS HURT WHEN YOU MAKE LOVE". NOBODY KNOWS WHO MADE THE CURSE, OR WHY.

The Aztecs had several sex goddesses, among them Tlazolteotl, goddess of lust and sexual misdeeds; Tlaco, goddess of sexual longing; and Teicu, goddess of sexual appetite.

A survey conducted by condom manufacturer Durex found that of all nations, Austrians engage in the most oral sex.

Vorarephilia is a sexual paraphilia characterized by the desire to eat, or be eaten by, others.

As surgery can cause nerve damage, some women with breast implants report a loss of sensitivity, while others claim increased sexual pleasure from having new breasts.

A study of 900 films over a four-year period found that scenes including sex and nudity did not increase a film's success.

COFFEE, TEA OR ME? IS A 1967 ACCOUNT OF THE SEXUAL EXPLOITS OF TWO AIRLINE STEWARDESSES, TRUDY BAKER AND RACHEL JONES. IN 2002, DONALD BAIN REVEALED THAT HE WAS THE REAL AUTHOR AND THAT THE PUBLISHER HAD HIRED TWO EASTERN AIRLINES STEWARDESSES TO POSE AS TRUDY AND RACHEL.

In seventeenth-century Spain, a woman could expose her breasts, but feet were considered sexual and it was illegal for anyone other than a woman's husband to see her bare feet.

Hugh Hefner published the first edition of *Playboy* magazine in America in December 1953; a nude Marilyn Monroe was the first *Playboy* centrefold.

During the Great Depression in America, "Tijuana bibles" were a popular form of entertainment: cheap stapled comics containing erotic stories.

According to one study, swallowing a partner's semen can lower blood pressure and, for women, lower risks of getting pre-eclampsia (a condition that causes high blood pressure during pregnancy and after labour), but only if it happens regularly before conception.

In sixteenth-century Canada, one aphrodisiac consisted of home-brewed alcohol with dried beaver testicles ground up into a fine powder.

"GLANS CONDOMS" – CAPS
COVERING THE HEAD OF
THE PENIS – WERE USED IN
ASIA BEFORE THE FIFTEENTH
CENTURY AND COULD
BE MADE OF OILED SILK
PAPER, LAMB INTESTINES,
TORTOISESHELL OR
ANIMAL HORN.

According to a survey of sex shop owners, the most popular flavour for edible underwear is cherry and the least popular is chocolate.

The symbols used for male and female represent Mars and Venus and consist of a shield and spear for the male, and a hand mirror for the female.

The word "sexennial" has nothing to do with sex; it means "occurring every six years", which we hope doesn't describe sex.

👄 Opposites attract because biologically we seek out potential mates with different DNA.

👄 Foods such as peaches, bananas, pine nuts, mussels, eels, horseradish, asparagus, cucumbers and onions are all believed to have aphrodisiac qualities.

IN 1524, MARCANTONIO
RAIMONDI PUBLISHED
16 ENGRAVINGS OF
CHARACTERS FROM
CLASSICAL HISTORY HAVING
SEX – AND WAS SENT TO
PRISON BY THE POPE.
HIS OFFICIAL CRIME WAS
COPYRIGHT VIOLATION,
BUT THE PORNOGRAPHIC
CONTENT WAS NO DOUBT
THE REAL ISSUE.

The area of the male brain responsible for sexual pursuit is two and a half times larger than the female equivalent, and it is fuelled by ten to 15 times the amount of testosterone.

The first reference to kissing comes from Sanskrit scriptures called the Vedas, dating back to 1500 BCE.

Research has shown that women's faces are found more attractive by both men and women in the days leading up to ovulation.

👄 The world's keenest users of the dating app Tinder are in the United States, followed by the UK and Brazil.

👄 The Condom Casino Tour is a programme that visits American universities to educate students about safe sex, through games such as Beer Goggle Black Jack and STD Bingo.

SCIENTIFIC STUDIES HAVE
SHOWN THAT HETEROSEXUAL
MEN WHO LOOKED AT PORN
OF TWO MEN AND ONE
WOMAN PRODUCED MORE
SPERM THAN THOSE WHO
LOOKED AT JUST WOMEN,
PERHAPS BECAUSE SEEING
COMPETITION MAKES
THE MAN INCREASE HIS
CHANCES OF IMPREGNATING
A FEMALE.

In Alabama, the sale of sex toys is a criminal offence. The law has been the subject of extensive litigation and has generated considerable national controversy.

A survey by ABC News revealed that cheating on a partner is the most common sexual fantasy for Americans.

Low levels of oestrogen, which occur during the menopause, can leave the vagina too dry for comfortable sex.

Men tend to reveal their underlying sexual motivation through their gaze, while women are less likely to express their thoughts so clearly in this way.

The sexologist Serenella Salomoni has claimed that when married couples remove the television from their bedroom, the frequency of sex doubles.

A 2015 STUDY SHOWED
THAT CLEAN-SHAVEN MALE
TINDER USERS GOT 37
PER CENT MORE MATCHES
THAN THEIR WHISKERED
COUNTERPARTS. IT'S SURELY
A COINCIDENCE THAT THE
STUDY WAS CONDUCTED BY
A RAZOR MANUFACTURER.

According to online journal *PLOS One*, people are less likely to consider something "disgusting" while in a state of sexual arousal.

According to *Runner's World* magazine, two out of three runners say they fantasize about sex while running.

"Falsies", or bra padding, designed to make the breasts look bigger or more pointed, became popular during the 1950s.

In 2013, ancient Greek statues of nude male figures caused shock when displayed in Qatar as part of an Olympic Games exhibition. They were covered with veils, then returned to Greece.

The fig leaf is associated with modesty. In the biblical Book of Genesis, Adam and Eve used fig leaves to cover their nakedness.

A PLASTER CAST FIG LEAF
WAS KEPT IN THE VICTORIA
AND ALBERT MUSEUM
DURING QUEEN VICTORIA'S
REIGN, TO COVER UP THE
GENITALS OF THE STATUE
OF MICHELANGELO'S DAVID
WHEN THE QUEEN OR OTHER
FEMALE DIGNITARIES VISITED.

The sadomasochistic novel *Venus in Furs*, first published in 1870, has been adapted for film five times, as well as giving its name to a Velvet Underground album.

Peyronie's disease is a condition in which a man's penis has a painfully abnormal curve when erect.

Eating a lot of white bread and other refined carbohydrates can be bad for a man's sex drive, reducing energy and testosterone levels.

Victorian women wore underwear with the crotch area open and exposed for hygiene reasons. Parisian cancan dancers advanced the trend for closed-crotch knickers.

Going for a run gets rid of stressors such as pent-up energy, tension and excess adrenaline, while releasing feel-good endorphins, therefore increasing sex drive.

THE *LITERARY REVIEW*'S BAD
SEX IN FICTION AWARD WAS
ESTABLISHED "TO DRAW
ATTENTION TO POORLY
WRITTEN, PERFUNCTORY OR
REDUNDANT PASSAGES OF
SEXUAL DESCRIPTION IN
MODERN FICTION". NOW
ALMOST 30 YEARS OLD, THE
AWARD SHOWS NO SIGN OF
RUNNING OUT OF SUITABLE
CANDIDATES.

The first couple to be shown in bed together in an animated series in America were Fred and Wilma Flintstone in *The Flintstones*.

In a *Glamour* magazine survey, 75 per cent of readers said they fantasized about their man dressing up as a fireman.

The eighteenth-century Venetian adventurer Casanova wrote about his powers of seduction and affairs in *The Story of My Life*, earning him the reputation as the world's greatest lover – and womanizer.

People who have sex approximately three times a week look several years younger than those who don't.

Experiencing "butterflies of love" sounds romantic, but in France the phrase *"papillon d'amour"* means having pubic lice.

BETWEEN 2007 AND 2015,
THE NUMBER OF AMERICANS
ADMITTED TO HOSPITAL
WITH INJURIES RELATING
TO SEX TOYS DOUBLED. A
PHENOMENON BELIEVED TO
BE CAUSED BY THE "*FIFTY
SHADES OF GREY* EFFECT".

The average vagina is 3 to 4 inches long but it can expand by 200 per cent when sexually aroused.

People who are risk takers or have a strong sense of adventure have a higher likelihood of cheating on their partner.

The orbicularis oris muscle is vital for kissing, as it allows the lips to pucker up.

Abstaining from any sexual activity for three weeks makes testosterone levels peak and boosts the libido, which can help to create the ultimate male orgasm.

An Italian study in 1990 showed that people who have just fallen in love can share symptoms experienced by sufferers of Obsessive Compulsive Disorder (OCD).

IN A 2010 STUDY, 85 PER
CENT OF MEN SAID THEIR
FEMALE PARTNERS HAD
HAD AN ORGASM AT THEIR
LAST SEXUAL ENCOUNTER,
WHILE ONLY 64 PER CENT OF
WOMEN REPORTED HAVING
HAD ONE.

Oscar Wilde's 1893 play *Salome* depicts probably the first striptease: the dance of the seven veils. This went on to become a standard in burlesque shows.

In the fifteenth century it was highly fashionable for European men to wear a codpiece – a flap positioned over their trousers which exaggerated the size of their manhood.

In the fifth century BCE, something called an olisbos, which we would call a dildo, was sold in the port of the Greek city of Miletus.

💋 *The Art of Love* by the Greek courtesan Philaenis is an ancient sex manual with information on aphrodisiacs and sex positions. It inspired the Roman poet Ovid to create his own manual a few centuries later.

💋 Ovid's version of *The Art of Love* includes advice for men such as "letting her miss you – but not for long" and for women, "trying young and older lovers".

AUTHORS IN THE
PROCEEDINGS OF THE
NATIONAL ACADEMY OF
SCIENCES CLAIM THAT
TORSO SHAPE IS THE
MOST IMPORTANT FACTOR
DETERMINING HOW
ATTRACTIVE WOMEN FIND
A MAN'S BODY, FOLLOWED
BY THE SIZE OF HIS FLACCID
PENIS AND HIS HEIGHT.

Strippers earn more money when ovulating, probably because of sexually stimulating pheromones they release at that stage of their menstrual cycles.

Horst Schultz holds the record for ejaculating the furthest distance, at a very impressive 18 feet and 9 inches.

Research has shown that women who feel confident about how their vulva looks find it easier to orgasm.

An ancient law in Alabama bans men from attempting to seduce "a chaste woman by means of temptation, arts, deception, flattery or a promise of marriage".

Lying down can reduce sensitivity to sound and smell, which could explain why other positions offer more sexual thrills.

Have you enjoyed this book? If so, find us on Facebook at **Summersdale Publishers**, on Twitter at **@Summersdale** and on Instagram and TikTok at **@summersdalebooks** and get in touch. We'd love to hear from you!

www.summersdale.com